Operating in the Power
of the Spirit

VOLUME 7

Operating *in the* Power *of the* Spirit

*I pray that from his glorious unlimited resources
He will give you mighty inner strength through
His Holy Spirit. Ephesians 3:16*

··

A 30-day Devotional Bible Study for Individuals or Groups.

··

Dr. Larry Keefauver

CREATION
H O U S E
Orlando, FL

OPERATING IN THE POWER OF THE SPIRIT by Larry Keefauver

Published by Creation House
Strang Communications Company
600 Rinehart Road
Lake Mary, FL 32746

Web site: http://www.creationhouse.com

Unless otherwise noted, all Scripture quotations are the Holy Bible, New Living Translation, copyright © 1996. Used by permission of Tyndale House Publishers, Inc., Wheaton, IL 60189. All rights reserved.

Printed in the United States of America

ISBN 0-88419-494-9

8901234 VP 8765432

Contents

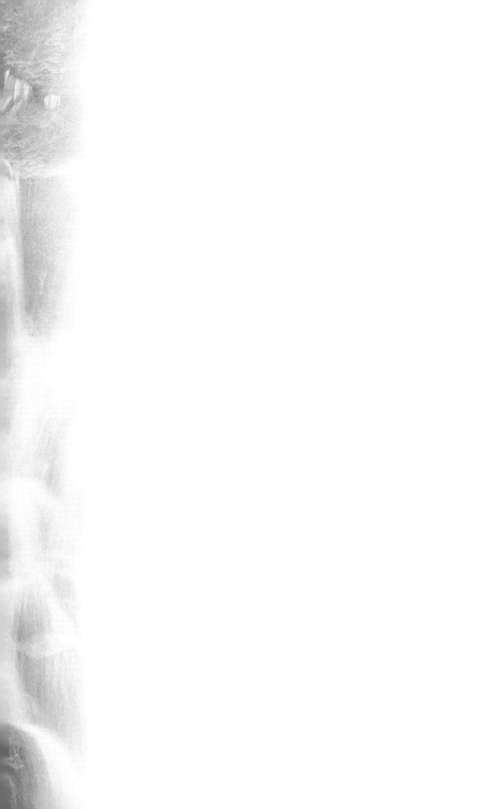

Introduction

Welcome to this devotional study on *Operating in the Power of the Holy Spirit* that will assist you in welcoming the Holy Spirit into your life. This is the seventh of eight devotional study guides related to the *Holy Spirit Encounter Bible*. Though not absolutely necessary, it is recommended that you obtain a copy of the *Holy Spirit Encounter Bible* for your personal use with this study guide. We make this recommendation because the same translation used in this guide, the *New Living Translation*, is also used in the *Holy Spirit Encounter Bible*.

It is also recommended that you choose the study guides in this series in the sequence that best meets your spiritual needs. So please don't feel that you must go through them in any particular order. Each study guide has been developed for individual, group, or class use.

Additional instruction has been included at the end of this guide for those desiring to use it in class or group settings.

Because the purpose of this guide is to help readers encounter the person of the Holy Spirit through the Scriptures, individuals going through it are invited to use it for personal daily devotional reading and study. Each daily devotional is structured to:

❖ Probe deeply into the Scriptures.

❖ Examine one's own personal relationship with the Holy Spirit.

❖ Discover biblical truths about the Holy Spirit.

❖ Encounter the person of the Holy Spirit continually in one's daily walk with God.

We pray this Bible study guide will serve you as an effective learning tool as you grow in fellowship with the wonderful third person of the triune God—the Holy Spirit. It is our prayer that, as you encounter the Holy Spirit daily in this devotional study, your life will be inspired to operate in the Spirit's power.

*T*hen he said to me, "This is what the Lord says to Zerubbabel: It is not by force nor by strength, but by my Spirit, says the Lord Almighty" (Zech. 4:6).

Apart from God's powerful Spirit, life is a desert blown to and fro by the scorching winds of depression, defeat, and death. But in Him, life springs up like an oasis to water parched, thirsty lands (Isa. 44:3).

DAY

The Holy
Spirit
Empowers

And there is victory in God's life-giving Spirit to overcome the trials of life. He transformed an ordinary man named Samson into a dynamic powerhouse who performed extraordinary feats of strength (Judg. 14). He transformed Solomon into the wisest man on earth, establishing the glory years of Israel's kingdom (1 Kings 4:29–34). And He transformed Peter to allow him to walk on water (Matt. 14:29).

By the power of God's Spirit Israel defeated their outnumbering enemies and entered into the Promised Land (Josh. 1:6–8).

With this witness of the Holy Spirit's power on His people in history, why do you still fall back upon your own strength? Complete the following sentence:

At times when I am weak, instead of trusting His Spirit, I _____

_____.

Now rank from one (1) to eight (8), the area of your life in which you need the Spirit's life-transforming power the most:

_____ Relationships

_____ Spiritual discipline

_____ Family

_____ Finances

_____ Marriage

_____ Future

_____ Work

_____ Other:_____

Are you willing to admit your weakness and yield to the Spirit's power? Until we confess our weakness, the Spirit won't choose to move powerfully in our lives. As long as we think we're strong without Him, He won't empower us to do His work. So we must either surrender fully to His power in order to be empowered—or remain powerless in our own strength.

Though humanly weak and powerless, you can encounter the Spirit's power and might because, in your weakness, He is strong (2 Cor. 12:9). Complete the following sentences:

My greatest spiritual weakness is _____

_____.

My greatest emotional weakness is _____

_____.

My greatest physical weakness is _____

_____.

My greatest mental weakness is _____

_____.

> *The only thing that keeps His power from flowing through you is your own unwillingness to surrender control of your life to His sovereign will.*

Understanding that all things are possible with God (Matt. 19:26), confess your inability and declare your availability to His Spirit. Then when you can't do what He requires, admit, "I can't, but You can."

Ask Yourself . . .

❖ Have you surrendered complete control to the Spirit's power?

❖ Where do you see His power at work in your life?

Write a prayer confessing your weakness and seeking the Spirit's power:

_____

_____

_____

*T*he earth was empty, a formless mass cloaked in darkness. And the Spirit of God was hovering over its surface (Gen. 1:2).

DAY 2
Empowered to Create

In the beginning, the ever-present Spirit of God hovered over the formless mass of the heavens and earth. For human beings to create, we must have something to work with—including our own bodies and our brains. But our Creator God (*El Ohim*), can create (*bara*) out of nothing (*ex nihilo*) to produce tangible physical material out of invisible spiritual things (Heb. 11:3).

God's Spirit hovered and brooded over His creation much like a hen protects her new chicks under the covering of her wings (Ps. 91:1–4). And just as He hovered over the earth in the beginning, the Spirit covers each new creation in Christ (2 Cor. 5:17). The Holy Spirit is always there to watch over and create new things in our lives (Isa. 43:19). "What this means is that those who become Christians become new persons. They are not the same anymore, for the old life is gone. A new life has begun!" (2 Cor. 5:17).

To check up on His new things empowering and changing your life, write an answer for each of the following questions:

What new thing is God's Spirit creating in your life right now? _____

_____

How have you experienced new things from the Spirit in the past? _____

_____

Now do a check on what keeps the Holy Spirit from creating new things in you. Check all that apply:

❑ Fear of losing control

❑ Lack of intimacy with the Spirit

❑ Hidden sin

❑ An inability to release the past

❑ Other: _____

Just as God's Spirit hovered over creation, so He covers you with His presence and protection while inspiring new change in your life. Every encounter with the Holy Spirit will bring newness and refreshing as He continually changes, renews, restores, and creates you to be more like Christ. So allow the Spirit to work creatively in you. He will give you new abilities and strength to face every situation in life.

> *The Holy Spirit indwells every believer with His creative power.*

Describe one way the Spirit's creative power has worked through you:

_____

_____

Finally, never forget that you are a human *being*—not a human *doing*. This means you were created by God's Spirit to be in relationship (or covenant) with Him. And because He is creative—you are creative.

The Spirit of God created you in His image to honor and worship Him, and because we are His creation, He loves you just the way you are. But He will continually watch over you to change and complete His restorative plan.

Ask Yourself . . .

❖ Are you allowing the Spirit of God to create and do new things in your life?

❖ Can you accept that God's Spirit created you and loves you as you are?

Write a prayer asking God's Spirit to fill you with His creative power:

_____

_____

_____

_____

_____

*T*hen at last they will respect and glorify the name of the Lord throughout the world. For he will come like a flood tide driven by the breath of the Lord (Isa. 59:19).

DAY 3

Empowered for Battle

Isaiah prophesied that the Messiah would come "like a flood tide driven by the breath (ruach) of the Lord" to destroy "His enemies according to their evil deeds" (v. 18). So no weapon formed against the Lord and His armies will ever prosper. Because the breath of God's Word (2 Thess. 2:8; Isa. 59:21) is unassailable, and God has already defeated every threatening foe, therefore, the battle you face is His, not yours.

When Joshua prepared to take Jericho, the Spirit of God told him the victory was Israel's before they marched to battle (Josh. 6:2.)! And God's Word of victory has also been spoken for you. So be strong and courageous. The outcome of every battle has already been secured!

Complete the following sentences about your battle.

The greatest battle I now face is _____
_____ .

About this battle I feel _____
_____ .

I feel myself losing the battle when _____
_____ .

I need to rely totally on the Spirit's power to _____
_____ .

Here are some power-filled "swords of the Spirit" that you can wield against the enemy every day (Eph. 6:10–18). Read each scripture and write it down in your own words. Then memorize them and use them to defeat the enemy by the power of His Spirit:

Swords of the Spirit	I declare . . .
Deuteronomy 28:13	_____
2 Samuel 22:31	_____
Psalm 107:20	_____

Lamentations 3:22–23 _____

John 16:24 _____

2 Corinthians 9:8 _____

Revelation 12:11 _____

Before you ever encounter the enemy, first encounter the Spirit of God.

> *God's mighty breath (*ruach*—Spirit) defeats the*
> *enemy as His Word comes out of your mouth.*

So, if God is for us, who can ever be against us? (Rom. 8:31). There is no reason to fear because "God has not given us a spirit of fear and timidity, but [a Spirit] of power, love, and self-discipline" (2 Tim. 1:7). Death has been defeated. Sin has been forgiven. Your past has been forgotten. And your future has been secured by the blood of Christ!

Ask Yourself . . .

❖ When will you stop fighting battles in your own strength and start declaring in the Spirit that the battle and victory belong to the Lord?

❖ How will you yield to the power of the Spirit when you face future battles?

Write a prayer seeking the Spirit's power to fight today's battles:

_____

_____

_____

_____

_____

*T*he Spirit of the Sovereign Lord is upon me, because the Lord has appointed me to bring good news to the poor. He has sent me to comfort the brokenhearted and to announce that captives will be released and prisoners will be freed. He has sent me to tell those who mourn that the time of the Lord's favor has come, and with it, the day of God's anger against their enemies. To all who mourn in Israel, he will give beauty for ashes, joy instead of mourning, praise instead of despair. For the Lord has planted them like strong and graceful oaks for his own glory (Isa. 61:1–3).

DAY 4
Empowered for Ministry

Because Jesus began His ministry with these words from Isaiah 61 (see Luke 4:18–19), the true nature of Spirit-led ministry is captured in this text. In it, the Lord declared that the Spirit's anointing on ministry would empower His servants to:

- ❖ Bring good news to the poor (both those who are poor spiritually [Matt. 5:3] and poor naturally [Luke 6:20] need the Good News).
- ❖ Comfort the brokenhearted (the comfort of the Holy Spirit for the heartache of defeat and sin: Matt. 5:4; Luke 6:21; John 14:16; 2 Cor. 1:3–11).
- ❖ And announce release to the captives and freedom to the prisoners (liberty and freedom for our lives). "Now, the Lord is the Spirit, and wherever the Spirit of the Lord is, he gives freedom" (2 Cor. 3:17).

Have you been allowing the Spirit to lead you in ministry as described in Isaiah's text? How has the anointing of the Holy Spirit ministered to, and operated through you to others? Complete these sentences:

When I was spiritually poor the Holy Spirit ministered _____

_____.

One way the Spirit has anointed me to minister to the poor is _____

_____.

The Spirit comforted my broken heart when _____

_____.

The Spirit ministered comfort through me when _____

_____.

The Spirit set me free to _____

_____.

The Spirit ministered liberty to others through me by _____

_____.

When the Spirit empowers you to minister, He entrusts you with a measure of His treasure, which is to be highly cherished. You become the bearer of His gifts, which, when delivered to others, showers them with a double portion of God's grace and everlasting joy (Isa. 61:2–7).

So true Spirit-led ministry is never a "position." It assumes the posture of a servant washing the feet of others while bearing God's good gifts (John 13).

> *The Spirit's empowering anointing for ministry takes broken vessels and sends them to others with the oil of His healing, joy, and praise.*

Ask Yourself . . .

❖ Are you willing to be broken and poured out by the Spirit in ministry?

❖ How is the Holy Spirit empowering you to minister in the church you attend?

Write a prayer asking God's Spirit to empower you for ministry:

_____

_____

_____

_____

_____

A *nd I will put my Spirit in you so you will obey my laws and do whatever I command (Ezek. 36:27).*

Without the Holy Spirit, it is impossible to obey God. In our own strength we all fall short of His glory (Rom. 3:23). But we aren't without hope, because God promised, "I will put my Spirit in you so you will obey my laws and do whatever I command" (Ezek. 36:27).

DAY 5
Empowered to Obey

Have you ever had a perfect day as a result of your own efforts? Of course not! Perfection is beyond the reach of humanity. Nevertheless, Jesus said, "But you are to be perfect, even as your Father in heaven is perfect" (Matt. 5:48). So Jesus apparently asked us to do the impossible. Why? Because doing anything that God commands is impossible without His Spirit. But as we draw near unto Him and receive His Spirit—we become more and more obedient—as we become more and more like Him!

Examine yourself. When do you find yourself the most disobedient? Check all that apply:

❑ When God asks me to do something I don't want to do.

❑ When God commands me to give something up.

❑ When God puts me through trials and tests.

❑ When God desires to minister and grow me in an area of my weakness.

❑ Other: _____

We receive the indwelling of the Holy Spirit through faith in Christ (Acts 2:38). So we have the gift of His Spirit within us to keep His commands once we are born again. All things become possible (Matt. 19:26; Phil. 4:13)!

God gave the Ten Commandments to Moses on Mount Saini as a basic revelation of man's inclination to sin. Which of them are most difficult for you to obey? Put an *x* on the line representing where you are (Exod. 20):

1. Do not worship other gods besides God.

_____
Hard   Easy

2. Do not make idols of any kind.

_____
Hard   Easy

3. Do not misuse the name of the Lord God.

_____
Hard   Easy

4. Observe the Sabbath.

Hard   Easy

5. Honor your father and mother.

Hard   Easy

6. Do not murder.

Hard   Easy

7. Do not commit adultery.

Hard   Easy

8. Do not steal.

Hard   Easy

9. Do not testify falsely against your neighbor.

Hard   Easy

10. Do not covet anything your neighbor owns.

Hard   Easy

We may all struggle from time to time in the tendencies of our human nature. But Jesus gave us the Spirit's nature. So the good news is that those who have God's Spirit dwelling within them have the power to keep all of God's commandments through Christ's higher law of love (1 Cor. 13). As the Holy Spirit faithfully compares our human nature with God's perfection—He convinces us to change.

> *Not only does the Spirit convict us of disobedience, He gives us the power to obey.*

Isn't it good to know that your obedience isn't dependent upon your own efforts, but on the power of God's Spirit working in you? But this also means that no one can take God's glory when they are empowered to obey, because obedience and grace go hand in hand as God matures our lives.

Ask Yourself . . .

❖ What is the Holy Spirit asking you to obey today?

❖ How is He empowering you to obey when your natural self wants to disobey?

Write a prayer asking the Holy Spirit to empower you to obey God in all things:

_____

_____

*T*hen he said to me, "Speak to these bones and say, 'Dry bones, listen to the word of the Lord! This is what the Sovereign Lord says: Look! I am going to breathe into you and make you live again! I will put flesh and muscles on you and cover you with skin. I will put breath into you, and you will come to life. Then you will know that I am the Lord'" (Ezek. 37:4–6).

DAY 6
Empowered for New Life

Are you truly tired of your old life? Hopefully you are, because there is a radically new, completely unique life available to you through the Holy Spirit. Ezekiel saw Israel's "old life" as a lifeless skeleton. Imagine your old life as a skeleton without muscles, organs, or skin. A skeleton does exist. But it's not alive. It wasn't until the Spirit asked Ezekiel: "Son of man, can these bones become living people again?" Then as God put flesh, muscles, and skin over the skeleton, the prophet got God's message—life is more than existence—it is living by the Spirit of God.

Our lives are like a valley of dry bones until the breath of God breathes life into us. Life comes from trusting the Life—Jesus Christ. He breathes into our dry bones the breath of new life, and *in Christ*, we become new creations (2 Cor. 5:17).

Write down below all the dead areas of your life that need the Spirit's power of new life:

_____

_____

_____

The Holy Spirit resurrects His new life out of the death we die to our old life. "For when we died with Christ we were set free from the power of sin. And since we died with Christ, we know we will also share his new life" (Rom. 6:7–8). That's why Paul writes, "I myself no longer live, but Christ lives in me. So I live my life in this earthly body by trusting in the Son of God, who loved me and gave himself for me" (Gal. 2:20).

Stop to think now about any areas of your life that were spiritually alive and empowered in the past, but have somehow become dead or dormant. List those areas and begin asking the Father for a fresh empowering from the Holy Spirit.

1. _____

2. _____

3. _____

4. _____

5. _____

When dry bones encounter the Holy Spirit, resurrection occurs.

You have been raised from the death of your sins to new life in Jesus Christ. So consider this: Alive in Christ, you no longer have to carry around the old bag of bones from your past, because each past sin, failure, and mistake can be discarded.

Ask Yourself . . .

❖ Are you ready to exchange the bag of old bones you have been carrying around for the new life of His Spirit?

❖ Whom do you need to tell about the reviving power of the Spirit for the dry bones of their lives?

Read Psalm 103, then write a prayer thanking God for the new life He gives you by His Spirit:

_____

_____

_____

_____

_____

*T*hen the Spirit took me up and brought me into the inner courtyard, and the glory of the Lord filled the Temple (Ezek. 43:5).

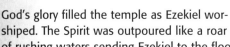

Empowered for Worship

The glory (*kabad*) of God is His indescribable brilliance, His outer garment of light and power. Where the Spirit of God is—His glory abides.

God's glory filled the temple as Ezekiel worshiped. The Spirit was outpoured like a roar of rushing waters sending Ezekiel to the floor as he fell to his face in awe (Ezek. 47).

When we encounter the glory of God, we worshipfully bow in the awe and fear of the Lord. In the presence of His glory, all darkness must flee. Every hidden place is brought to light. No bondage can remain. The spirit of heaviness is replaced by the garment of praise. Every idol is shattered, because God's Spirit will never share His glory with any other.

When the Holy Spirit lifts us up into the inner court of His holiness, the glory of God fills the temple of our lives. God's glory transforms us continually (2 Cor. 3:18). His glory fills us with an unceasing desire to pray and worship and anoints our lips with praise for the honor of His name: "Amen! Blessing and glory and wisdom and thanksgiving and honor and power and strength belong to our God forever and forever. Amen!" (Rev. 7:12).

Describe a time when you encountered the glory of God's Spirit:

_____

_____

Now complete the following statement:

Lord, forgive me for claiming Your glory when I_____

_____.

You must never claim or try to grasp His glory for yourself, because it is the nature of His glory to grasp and change us. When we put ourselves on the throne of our lives, His glory departs.

> *If you touch God's glory, the Spirit's power will depart.*

When the glory of God fills the temple of your life, no other presence matters. No other life exists. No other honor can be given except to that name which has been glorified above every other name—Jesus.

Make this spiritual vow: *I will never accept glory.*

Say this aloud a number of times. Ask the Spirit to empower you to keep this vow.

Because we have been united with Christ and have put on His glory, God's Spirit clothes us with His glory (Rom. 15:7). But His glory won't cover old garments. So it is up to us to take off our old garb of religion, self, pride, and sin. It is then, as we stand complete in Him, that His Spirit fills our temples and empowers us to worship.

Are you ready to shine in His glory and none of your own? "Those who are wise will shine bright as the sky, and those who turn many to righteousness will shine like stars forever" (Dan. 12:3). When we worship the Lord in Spirit and in truth (John 4:24) we reflect Jesus' glory like stars in the sky.

Ask Yourself . . .

❖ Do you mirror the glory of Christ's reflection in your life as a result of being filled by His Spirit?

❖ Will you vow never to touch His glory?

Write a prayer asking the Holy Spirit to clothe you in the power of His glory:

_____

_____

_____

_____

_____

*A*nd I will never again turn my back on them, for I will pour out my Spirit upon them, says the Sovereign Lord (Ezek. 39:29).

DAY 8

Empowered for Covenant Relationship

Only the Spirit can bring us into covenant with God. *Covenant* means "relationship." It is an agreement between God and man sealed by the blood of Christ. God's New Covenant is written by His Spirit upon our hearts (Jer. 31:31).

With the New Covenant comes an eternal promise: "And I will give them singleness of heart and put a new spirit within them. I will take away their hearts of stone and give them tender hearts instead, so they will obey my laws and regulations" (Ezek. 11:19).
"But this is the New Covenant I will make with the people of Israel on that day . . . I will put my laws in their minds, and I will write them on their hearts. I will be their God, and they will be my people" (Jer. 31:33).

On the heart below, write some of the new feelings and attitudes the Spirit has put within you:

Our covenant relationship with God doesn't set aside our responsibility to read, study, learn, meditate, and memorize His covenant Word. But it does ensure our ability to understand and obey His Word.

Jesus fulfills God's Word (the Law) in and through us by His Spirit (see Matt. 5:17–20; Rom. 6:1–23; Gal. 5:1–6). The people tried to obey it under the Old Covenant, but they couldn't because of the weakness of the flesh. Under our new and better covenant, however, those empowered by the Spirit don't need to "try" obedience—we can trust Jesus Christ for the will and power to obey.

Are you trying or trusting? Mark where you are in each of the following areas with an *x*.

I try to obey.	I trust Jesus for power to obey.

I struggle to obey God's Word by effort.	I keep the Word by grace.

I work at faith.	My works are the fruit of faith in Jesus.

The result of the New Covenant in Christ is that we live by the power of the Holy Spirit through faith in Him, knowing that by grace, not our own efforts, we can obey God (Eph. 2:8–10).

Obedience becomes the heart's desire under our new and better covenant because it is born out of our love for Jesus Christ (John 14:21). So rejoice! Because today under the New Covenant the Spirit empowers us to love and trust God even when we don't feel like it or understand it with our natural mind—because He first loved us (1 John 4:7–17).

Ask Yourself . . .

❖ Are you *trying* to obey, or completely *trusting* Jesus to empower you to obey by His Spirit?

❖ In what new ways is the Spirit teaching you to trust Jesus?

Write a prayer asking for the Spirit's power to trust Christ and surrender your own efforts of trying to obey Him in your own strength:

_____

_____

_____

_____

_____

*T*hen the Lord summoned me and said, *"Those who went north have vented the anger of my Spirit there" (Zech. 6:8).*

Fatigue—it seems to be everywhere. Everyone complains about being tired, overworked, stressed, and too busy. Rushing here and there, we push too much into our schedules while neglecting a time to rest in the Spirit.

What fatigues you the most? Circle all your most common sources:

Empowered for Rest

Overwork	Stress	Family
Ministry	Repressed Anger	Sickness
Emotional Pain	Other: _____	

The exiles of Israel returned to the Promised Land in the Book of Zechariah to rebuild their temple and to rest in God. Their exile in Babylon represented a time of struggle, slavery, work, and no time to keep the Law, including its commanded Sabbath Day rest.

The same is true of those outside of Christ today. They toil and struggle and are restless in soul. But those who come home and allow the Holy Spirit to make them His temples receive His power to serve the Lord and find rest for their souls. The invitation of Jesus promises, "Come to me, all of you who are weary and carry heavy burdens, and I will give you rest. Take my yoke upon you. Let me teach you, because I am humble and gentle, and you will find rest for your souls" (Matt. 11:28–29).

The Holy Spirit empowers us to rest, but sometimes we don't. What robs you of the Spirit's rest? Check all that apply:

- ❏ My work
- ❏ My financial burdens
- ❏ Raising my children
- ❏ My marriage
- ❏ My church work
- ❏ My hobbies

The end result of *trying* instead of *trusting* God's Spirit is physical, mental, and spiritual fatigue. Our own efforts land us in the Babylon of our own slavery and exile where we find ourselves estranged and cut off from God's rest.

> *Until the Spirit gives you the power to rest, every outer conflict will disturb your inner peace and rest.*

But there is hope. Like Israel, you can return from exile to God's Promised Land of rest and peace in Jesus Christ. No matter what whirlwind of draining activities swirls about you, the Spirit will give you inner rest.

Ask Yourself . . .

❖ At the center of life's hurricanes, do you know the rest and calm His Spirit brings?

❖ What rest-robbers do you need to surrender to the Holy Spirit?

Write a prayer seeking the filling of the Spirit's peace and rest:

_____

_____

_____

_____

_____

*T*hen after I have poured out my rains again, I will pour out my Spirit upon all people. Your sons and daughters will prophesy. Your old men will dream dreams. Your young men will see visions. In those days, I will pour out my Spirit even on servants, men and women alike (Joel 2:28–29).

A power-filled river flows from the throne of God that floods and overflows your life. A fountain bubbles up deep within you. A shower rains on your desert. A spring of living waters makes an oasis out of your wilderness and a lush forest for your thirsty

Empowered for Outpouring

soil. God's promise echoing throughout the Old Testament is this: The outpouring of God's Spirit is coming upon young and old, sons and daughters, men and women—servants everywhere. (See Joel 2:28–29.)

The Spirit's outpouring can't be earned by the religious, the privileged wealthy, the strong, or the powerful.

> *Only those desperate for the power of the Spirit's outpouring will be ready to receive it.*

The outpouring of the Holy Spirit comes upon the different types of people listed below. Place a check mark in each box that represents you:

❑ The thirsty and dry

❑ The poor in spirit

❑ Those who are humble servants

❑ Those listening for His Spirit

❑ Those needing rest

❑ Those weak and powerless

❑ Those eager and waiting

❑ Those loving God, neighbor, and self

The outpouring of the Spirit comes upon everyone whose needy cries reach heaven from where His blessing of Pentecost is poured forth (Acts 1–2). He pours when we humble ourselves to His will, not the other way around.

In what ways have you tried to force the Holy Spirit to outpour His power into your life? List three ways you have tried to manipulate, control, or force the Spirit to act powerfully on your behalf. Also describe how He responded:

1. _____

2. _____

3. _____

Our sovereign God pours out His Spirit in love and grace resulting in visions, dreams, and prophecy. And He gives us His power to fulfill what He has shown. But the Spirit's outpouring can never be forced, rushed, manipulated, or controlled.

Ask Yourself . . .

❖ Have you encountered the Spirit's outpouring of dreams, visions, and prophecy in your life?

❖ If you have ever tried to force the Spirit to act, are you willing to admit it and submit your life totally to God?

Write a prayer thanking the Holy Spirit for the outpouring of His power in in your life. Pray for Pentecost's outpouring.

_____

_____

_____

_____

_____

*O*n the day of Pentecost, seven weeks after Jesus' resurrection, the believers were meeting together in one place. Suddenly, there was a sound from heaven like the roaring of a mighty windstorm in the skies above them, and it filled the house where they were meeting. Then, what looked like flames or tongues of fire appeared and settled on each of them. And everyone present was filled with the Holy Spirit and began speaking in other languages, as the Holy Spirit gave them this ability (Acts 2:1–4).

DAY 11
Fiery Power

When God's Spirit was poured out at Pentecost, His fiery outpouring was accompanied by His supernatural power. "But when the Holy Spirit has come upon you, you will receive power and will tell people about me everywhere" (Acts 1:8).

The Greek word for power is *dunamis*, which means "the miracle-working, dynamic power of God." So when the fiery Spirit moves in dynamic power— miracles of salvation, healings, deliverances, and abundant provision from God occur among His believers giving powerful witness to unbelievers of the gospel's truth. Zechariah 4:6 says, "It is not by force nor by strength, but by my Spirit" (4:6).

When the Holy Spirit's fiery power was released in the early church, great and wondrous things happened. The following signs of His presence occurred in the Book of Acts. Circle any of them you have seen in your own life and church:

When the Spirit's power is released, people . . .

Are saved	Become generous	Get their needs met
Become joyful	Witness boldly	Perform signs and wonders
Praise God	Fear God	Are baptized
Meet together often for worship		Share the Lord's Supper
Enjoy the good will of others		

The fiery power (dunamis) of Pentecost is the miracle-working, dynamic force of the Holy Spirit to make us bold in witness and to operate in mighty signs that confirm the Word of Christ (see Mark 16:15–18).

Now let's briefly review how the Holy Spirit actually manifested His power through Christ's believers in Acts. Here are some examples. Write down how the Spirit's power was demonstrated:

Acts 2:43–47 _____

Acts 3:1–10 _____

Acts 4:1–22 _____

Acts 4:23–31 _____

Acts 5:1–16 _____

Acts 6:7 _____

Acts 6:10 _____

Acts 7:54–56 _____

Acts 9:1–19 _____

Acts 9:31 _____

Acts 10:44–47 _____

Acts 11:27–28 _____

Acts 13:1–5 _____

Acts 13:6–12 _____

Acts 19:1–7 _____

An encounter with the fire of the Holy Spirit radically changes your life. The fire of His Acts 2 outpouring at Pentecost began a movement of God in history that literally turned the world upside down (Acts 17:6).

Ask Yourself . . .

❖ How have the manifestations of the Spirit's power operated in your life?

❖ What hinders the Spirit's power from working His signs and wonders through you? Through your church?

Write a prayer asking God to pour out His fiery Spirit of dunamis *power upon you:*

_____

_____

O n the day of Pentecost, seven weeks after Jesus' resurrection, the believers were meeting together in one place. Suddenly, there was a sound from heaven like the roaring of a mighty windstorm in the skies above them, and it filled the house where they were meeting. Then, what looked like flames or tongues of fire appeared and settled on each of them. And everyone present was filled with the Holy Spirit and began speaking in other languages, as the Holy Spirit gave them this ability (Acts 2:1-4).

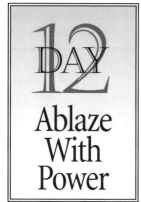

DAY 12
Ablaze With Power

Does ablaze by the Spirit of God describe your life? Jesus baptizes us in the Holy Spirit and fire (Matt. 3:11). Flames or tongues of fire rested on the believers at Pentecost (Acts 2). And Jesus admonishes us to be fiery hot for Him (Rev. 3:15-16). So, ablaze by the Spirit should fit your general description in Him.

God's fiery presence indwells our lives—which are the temples of the Holy Spirit (1 Cor. 3:16; 6:19). That's why Jesus said we would shine as lights in the world: "You are the light of the world—like a city on a mountain, glowing in the night for all to see. Don't hide your light under a basket! Instead, put it on a stand and let it shine for all" (Matt. 5:14-15).

How brightly is your light shining for Jesus Christ? Below is a fiery flame. Near it, the areas of your life that should be on fire for Christ by the power of His Spirit are listed. Place a check mark beside each area that you believe is flaming brightly. Then circle any area that still needs to be ignited by the Holy Spirit's fire in your life:

❑ Prayer life   ❑ Faith

❑ Worship   ❑ Giving

❑ Witnessing   ❑ Serving

❑ Relationships   ❑ Emotions

❑ Work   ❑ Thoughts

❑ Ministry   ❑ Leisure

❑ Other: _____

Jesus baptizes you with the fire of Pentecost, but it is up to you to stay ablaze. The coals of His burning must be constantly stirred in your heart through prayer and the Word. Are you burning brightly with the Spirit's power? Or are you cold, unlit, and unseen by those who need to see His light in you?

Write what you believe is the greatest area of your life that needs to be set ablaze by the power of God's Spirit.

_____

_____

_____

Daniel prophesied: "Those who are wise will shine as bright as the sky, and those who turn many to righteousness will shine like stars forever" (Dan. 12:3). And the only way to shine like the stars is to be set on fire by the Holy Spirit.

Unlit coals can't warm cold hands or cook steaks for a hungry crowd, and a room is dark until a candle is lit. Is the Spirit's fire cooking you as living bread for others?

> *Your life is without purpose until it is set ablaze by the Spirit's power.*

Ask Yourself . . .

❖ Do you mirror the glory of Christ ablaze in His presence?

❖ Where is your light shining brightest for Christ?

Write a prayer seeking the baptism of the Spirit's fiery power on your life:

_____

_____

_____

_____

_____

*S*o now there is no condemnation for those who belong to Christ Jesus. For the power of the life-giving Spirit has freed you through Christ Jesus from the power of sin that leads to death (Rom. 8:1–2).

The powerful, life-giving Spirit of God has freed you from all condemnation! That's why Paul launches into his description of life in the Spirit with this cry of freedom in Romans 8. Living in the Spirit frees you from being controlled by the sin that took place in your past. Because the Christian life is not about your past—it has been cleansed by the blood of Christ!

DAY 13
Living in the Spirit's Power

So if a Christian does live in condemnation, it is because of a personal choice, not because he must. Once we are born again, the only condemnation we encounter are the lies and accusations the enemy uses in his attacks. So don't accept them. Don't accept the condemnation.

Read each of the following passages, then jot down what they say about condemnation:

Galatians 5:1–15 _____

1 John 3:18–24 _____

Revelation 12:10–12 _____

Paul writes that "you are not controlled by your sinful nature. You are controlled by the Spirit if you have the Spirit of God living in you" (Rom. 8:9).

> *To live in the Spirit is to be controlled, motivated, and empowered by the Spirit, free from the controlling influence of sin.*

But of course, sin will always battle. So rank in order of influence those worldly forces that attack you and try to take control: (Rank from the strongest attack (1) to the least (9).)

_____ Lusts and sexual passions

_____ Substance abuse

_____ Doubts and fears

_____ Money and materialism

_____ Other people

_____ Religious legalism

_____ Work and ambition

_____ Pride and status

_____ Other:

The Holy Spirit has broken the bondage of condemnation and control over your life. So none of the above-listed sinful tendencies can dominate your life. You are free to live in the Spirit: "But if the Holy Spirit controls your mind, there is life and peace" (Rom. 8:6).

Now list seven ways the Holy Spirit has given you new life and peace:

1. _____

2. _____

3. _____

4. _____

5. _____

6. _____

7. _____

When you live in the Holy Spirit, your sinful nature no longer controls your thoughts and actions as you continually encounter His presence in new life and peace (Rom. 8:13).

So stop cowering in condemnation and start saying, "I am a child of God and is therefore no condemnation in me who is in Christ. I belong to God's very own family. The Holy Spirit tells me so. I am free from all condemnation in Jesus Christ!"

Ask Yourself . . .

❖ Have you been set free from condemnation to become Spirit-controlled?

❖ Where in your life do you need to surrender personal control and begin living totally under the Spirit's power?

Write a prayer thanking God's Spirit for setting you free from the power of sin:

_____

_____

*J*ohn *baptized you with water, but in just a few days you will be baptized with the Holy Spirit. . . . But when the Holy Spirit has come upon you, you will receive power and will tell people about me everywhere—in Jerusalem, throughout Judea, in Samaria, and to the ends of the earth (Acts 1:5, 8).*

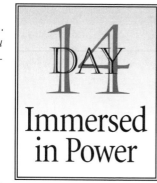

DAY 14
Immersed in Power

Baptism means "to be immersed in water." So how is one baptized in the Spirit? Where is the water? The water of Spirit baptism is the river of God that flows from His throne into our lives. His river produces a perpetual flow within us that fills us with the power and presence of God every moment of our lives.

You will receive power. Jesus promises that there is power in God's river. What power are you seeing evidenced in your life as a result of being immersed in His river? Read Acts 2, which chronicles a number of evidences of the Spirit's power available through God's river. Then write down every evidence you find:

In the Spirit's baptism, there is power to . . .

1. _____

2. _____

3. _____

4. _____

5. _____

6. _____

7. _____

8. _____

[To confirm what you've found, read again Acts 2:4, 41–47.]

Is your life power-filled or powerless? Check all the evidences of the Holy Spirit's power present now in your life:

❑ Signs and wonders   ❑ Holiness

❑ Gifts of the Spirit   ❑ Purity

❑ Hunger and thirst for God   ❑ Sharing with others

❑ Speaking in other languages   ❑ Love

❏ Deeper prayer, praises, and worship

❏ Great joy and generosity

❏ Boldly witnessing   ❏ Other:_____

> *The Spirit's power in your life empowers you to witness—*
> *sharing the good news of Jesus Christ with others.*

Are you a reluctant witness or a bold, empowered witness? Remember that the Holy Spirit will even give you the words you need when you witness (Luke 12:12). What keeps the power to witness shut off in your life? If you aren't witnessing boldly, check the things listed below that keep you from being a powerful witness:

❏ Fear   ❏ Embarrassment

❏ Ignorance   ❏ Too busy

❏ Disobedience   ❏ Not willing to get involved with unbelievers

❏ Other: _____

Ask Yourself . . .

❖ What evidences of being immersed in the Spirit's power are you seeing in your life?

❖ With whom do you need to be sharing the gospel?

Write a prayer asking Jesus to immerse you in the Spirit's power:

_____

_____

_____

_____

_____

*T*he Spirit gives special faith to another, and to someone else the power to heal the sick (1 Cor. 12:9).

The power to heal the sick never resides in a human being. It always rests in the power and sovereignty of God, because it resides in His very nature.

Power to Heal

Read the following passages below and jot down what they say about God and His nature that heals:

Exodus 15:26 _____

_____

Psalm 103:3 _____

Psalm 107:20 _____

Isaiah 53:5; 1 Peter 2:24 _____

Isaiah 61:1–3; Psalm 147:3 _____

Jeremiah 30:17 _____

Malachi 4:2 _____

Mark 2:32–34 _____

Mark 6:53–56 _____

Some who are given the gift of healing are mistakenly called "faith healers," or "healing evangelists." But the truth is that no human can heal. Only God can heal. So when someone is healed through a willing vessel operating in the Spirit's power, both the one healed, and the one ministering the gift, should give all glory to God!

Have you ever witnessed anyone healed by the power of God? If so, describe how God's Spirit moved to heal them:

_____

_____

The gift of the power to heal comes from the Holy Spirit and ministers through willing believers who serve as vessels of God's grace and power to heal whomever He pleases.

36

The Spirit knows the deep needs of people and what in them needs healing. And His spiritual gift of healing may be ministered in a number of ways. Below is a list of some of them. Circle those ways you have experienced personally or witnessed in the body of Christ:

Laying on of hands (Mark 16:18)

Praying for the sick (James 5:15)

Confession of sins (James 5:16)

Exercising faith in Christ (Luke 7:1–10; Mark 5:34)

Believing and trusting His Word to heal (Ps. 107:20)

Obeying *Jehovah-Rapha*—the God who heals you (Exod. 15:26)

Commanding healing in Jesus' name (Acts 3:4–8)

Applying the blood of Jesus Christ (1 Pet. 2:24)

Anointing with oil (James 5:14)

Other: _____

Does everyone touched by one who ministers in the gift of healing instantly receive physical healing? No. Anyone who ministers in the power of any of the gifts of the Spirit realizes that God can't be manipulated or controlled. In Him is healing, but He operates according to His plan—not ours. He not only wants to heal us, but He wants us to have faith and grow in understanding in our experiences. And remember: Everyone who lives and dies in Christ will one day be raised perfectly healed—body, soul, and spirit (1 Cor. 15). So every Christian will receive God's healing eventually.

Ask Yourself . . .

❖ Whose healing do you need to be praying for?

❖ In what ways have you encountered healing from the Holy Spirit?

Write a prayer asking God's Spirit to use you to bring healing into the lives of others:

_____

_____

_____

*H*e [the Holy Spirit] gives one person the power to perform miracles (1 Cor. 12:10).

Miracles are extraordinary events powerfully performed by God beyond the scope of natural events. They are a supernatural manifestation of the power of God.

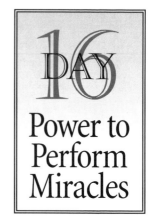

Power to Perform Miracles

The Holy Spirit did mighty miracles in the early church to demonstrate His power and salvation. Read the following Scriptures and jot down what they say about miracles:

Acts 2:22 _____

Acts 2:43 _____

Acts 4:29–30 _____

Acts 5:12 _____

Acts 6:8 _____

Acts 8:6 _____

Acts 8:13 _____

Acts 14:3 _____

Acts 15:12 _____

Filled with the power of the Spirit (Luke 4:14), Jesus performed many miracles throughout His earthly ministry. And He promised that His followers would do even greater miracles than Him (John 14:12). God didn't stop working them in the early church. So know, as Jesus' follower, that He wants to work miracles through you!

God demonstrated His power and presence throughout the Bible through various miracles. List five of the greatest miracles you can recall:

1. _____

2. _____

3. _____

4. _____

5. _____

God is a miracle-working God from the miracle of creation—to the Exodus; from

Sinai and the wilderness—to Jericho; from the slaying of Goliath—to the Exile and Return; from the miracles that Jesus performed—to the Resurrection; and from the miracle of Pentecost—to the miracles of the early church—and beyond.

Describe a miracle that you have experienced through the power of the Holy Spirit.

_____

_____

Have you ever encountered the gift of miracles working through you to minister to the body of Christ? Describe one such time:

_____

_____

> *Miracles are signs used by the Holy Spirit to point people to the miracle worker—Jesus Christ.*

As with the gift of healing power, the power to perform miracles doesn't reside in a human being. Such power comes from God's Spirit. His miracles manifest His glory for all to see. The purpose of signs (miracles) revealed in Acts 2:43 shows that, "A deep sense of awe came over them all, and the apostles performed many miraculous signs and wonders."

So miracles inspire us to reverence, praise and give glory to God.

Ask Yourself . . .

❖ What miraculous things have been empowered by His Spirit recently in your life?

❖ What miracles are you praying for now?

Write a prayer asking God's Spirit to work miraculously in the lives of those in His body:

_____

_____

*A*t that time the Spirit of the Lord will come upon you with power, and you will prophesy with them. You will be changed into a different person (1 Sam. 10:6). He [the Holy Spirit] gives one person the power to perform miracles, and to another the ability to prophesy . . . Let love be your highest goal, but also desire the special abilities the Spirit gives, especially the gift of prophecy (1 Cor. 12:10; 14:1).

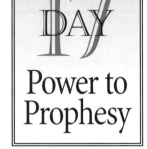

DAY 17
Power to Prophesy

In Hebrew, the word for *prophet* (*nabi*) means to be a "mouthpiece," or a "spokesman" for God. In other words, a prophet delivers the "Word of the Lord." Prophecy brings conviction, repentance, and worship to the body of Christ.

Saul's life was changed when he was empowered by the Spirit to prophesy. Have you ever had a similar prophetic experience that changed your life? If so please describe it:

_____

_____

Encountering God's prophetic Word is described in 1 Corinthians 14:24–25. Read that passage, then list all that happens in the body when prophesy comes from the Lord:

1. _____

2. _____

3. _____

4. _____

5. _____

This passage reveals that the main purpose of prophecy is to bring unbelievers to repentance and to a point of worshiping God. So the gift of prophecy is God's special ability to communicate His urgent truth through a yielded person in a Spirit-anointed word.

But persons claiming to minister under a prophetic anointing need to submit to the test of prophets. The criteria for examining the authenticity of a prophetic word are given in the following passages. Read each one carefully and write down what it says.

Prophetic Trust Test

1 Corinthians 14:29–33 _____

1 Corinthians 14:39–40 _____

1 John 4:1–6 _____

Deuteronomy 13:1–5 _____

Deuteronomy 18:15–22 _____

Notice that false prophecy is judged harshly by the Lord. And that whatever a prophet says must come to pass, or that person is a false prophet. In other words, the Word from the Lord is always 100 percent true. So a person who claims to be a prophet and only speaks truth part of the time may be nothing more than an intellect-driven preacher, or even a psychic that utters words from other spirits. That's why Paul encourages us to not quench the Holy Spirit and not to scoff, but to test all prophecies (1 Thess. 5:19–20).

> *When ministering a prophetic word from the Lord, the Spirit of God prompts and anoints a person to speak His Word.*

So the prompting comes from the Holy Spirit, not from intellect, events, circumstances, needs, wants, or human ideas. Because a prophecy is a "God idea" not just a "good idea."

Since a true prophetic word comes from the Lord, it will always conform to God's Word and will never contradict Scripture. And the purpose of that word will always be consistent with the purpose of God's Word. Read 2 Timothy 3:16–17 and jot down what the Word will produce:

_____

_____

Describe a time when the Spirit inspired you with a word that encouraged, edified, and blessed another person's life:

_____

_____

Ask Yourself . . .

❖ What is the Spirit prophetically revealing to you?

❖ How are you proclaiming God's Word through both your words and actions?

> *Write a prayer asking the Holy Spirit to reveal His Word to you so you might prophetically speak and act out His Word:*

_____

_____

A nd the Holy Spirit helps us in our distress. For we don't even know what we should pray for, nor how we should pray. But the Holy Spirit prays for us with groanings that cannot be expressed in words. And the Father who knows all hearts knows what the Spirit is saying, for the Spirit pleads for us believers in harmony with God's own will (Rom. 8:26–27).

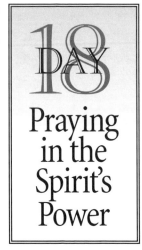

DAY 18
Praying in the Spirit's Power

In our own strength, we can only pray, "Lord, be merciful to me a sinner." But in the power of the Spirit, we can ask anything in the name of Jesus (John 15:16).

When the Holy Spirit prays through us He goes way beyond our human ability to express what He desires in human words. The Holy Spirit may pray through us with tongues or groanings that go deeper than mere words. He intercedes in us for our needs, and through us for the needs of others.

When the Spirit of God uses us to pray for others (intercession), we become God's vessel for implementing His will in their lives. How? God responds to prayer because it is His ordained vehicle for implementing His will on the earth. That's why Jesus teaches us, "I also tell you this: If two of you agree down here on earth concerning anything you ask, my Father in heaven will do it for you" (Matt. 18:19).

Ephesians 6:18 gives us guidance concerning how we are to intercede for others. Read this verse now, then complete the following sentences as they relate to you after each of Paul's instructions:

Pray at all times.

Daily I pray _____

The times I need to pray are _____

Pray on every occasion.

What circumstances prompt you to pray immediately? _____
_____

In what situations do you need to being praying? _____
_____

Pray in the power of the Holy Spirit.

What demonstrations of the Spirit's power have you witnessed as a result of

prayer? _____

List all the ways the Spirit prays through you: _____

_____

Be alert and persistent in your prayers.

What dangers has the Spirit alerted you to pray about? _____

_____

What needs of others has the Spirit alerted you to pray for?_____

_____

In what ways is the Spirit teaching you to be more patient and persistent in

your praying?_____

Pray for all Christians everywhere.

What believers are you to pray for in your city, in the nation, and in the world?

_____

How has the Spirit been leading you to pray for all Christians?_____

_____

Ask Yourself . . .

❖ What changes in your prayer life does the Spirit desire you to make?

❖ When you pray in the power of the Spirit, what evidences of His power do
you see in your life, your family, and your church?

Write a prayer of intercession that the Holy Spirit desires you to pray:

_____

_____

_____

_____

*F*or when we brought you the Good News, it was not only with words but also with power, for the Holy Spirit gave you full assurance that what we said was true (1 Thess. 1:5).

Powerful Assurance

The good news of the Spirit-led life is that the Holy Spirit will enable you to live with power and holiness. And that you can be assured that He is working in you to complete His plan for your life (Phil. 1:6).

So you can walk forward with the Holy Spirit in boldness and confidence. At times, you will not fully understand why the Spirit is directing you in a certain way. But you can be assured that His plan for your life is for your very best (Jer. 29:11–12).

Complete these sentences:

In the Spirit, I am most confident of _____

_____.

Where I lack confidence in the Holy Spirit is_____

_____.

My prayer for confidence is _____

_____.

When you *know that you know* that the Holy Spirit is empowering your life with confidence and assurance, then you will live for Christ with great boldness. Too often your witness may be compromised because you are not assured of His power at work in your decisions. How can you tap the assurance of His power at work in every decision of life?

Here are some steps the Holy Spirit will use to build assurance and confidence in your decisions so that you have the power to make right choices.

- ❖ Compare every choice you have with the person, nature, and attributes of God.
- ❖ Ask the question, "What would God's Spirit have me do?" Search the Scriptures for guidance.
- ❖ Listen to the voice of the Holy Spirit through the Word, prophecy, prayer, and the fellowship of the saints.
- ❖ Pray that the Spirit baptizes you with the power and strength to do what is righteous and to stand firm against any attack.

❖ Count the cost of righteousness. Be prepared for rejection, persecution, and suffering for Jesus' sake.

❖ Be prepared to wait for your reward or harvest. Assurance is not strengthened by immediate rewards from God, but by His inner peace and joy that comes from knowing and following Jesus.

Now carefully look over the above list and circle every step that needs to be taken in your upward call of Christ. Ask the Lord to baptize you with assurance and power in the Holy Spirit to make right choices.

Ask Yourself . . .

❖ Are you willing to surrender all to the control and leading of the Holy Spirit?

❖ Will you walk in the power of the Holy Spirit making right choices regardless of the worldly cost you may pay?

Write a prayer asking the Holy Spirit to build powerful assurance and confidence in your life:

_____

_____

_____

_____

_____

*D*o not stifle the Holy Spirit (1 Thess. 5:19).

Day 20

Don't Stifle the Spirit's Power

To stifle or quench the Spirit is like throwing cold water on a fire or extinguishing the flame of love with rejection. He doesn't force us to accept His leading. So whenever the Spirit desires to move in our lives, we must give Him liberty and freedom.

We can either follow and obey the Spirit's leading, or resist and stifle His guidance, counsel, and power. Think of it this way: A garden hose can freely allow water to pass through it, or it can be crimped. The more it is bent and knotted, the more the flow of water is stifled, or restricted. In the same way, the living water of God's Spirit flows through your life like a river (John 7:37–39). And it is up to you to yield completely, or to crimp and stifle His flow.

How do you respond to the Holy Spirit moving powerfully in your life or in the lives of those around you? Below are some of the different ways the Spirit moves. Jot down where you are right now in giving Him freedom:

When the Spirit . . .	My response is to . . .
Rejoices in me	_____
Releases His gifts through me	_____
Witnesses through me	_____
Speaks through me	_____
Convicts me	_____
Worships through me	_____
Loves the unlovely through me	_____
Serves the least of these through me	_____

Paul encouraged the Thessalonians not to scoff at prophecies but to test what is said and to hold onto what is good (1 Thess. 5:19–21). The Holy Spirit will confirm His Word through a number of excellent ways (Acts 15:8). But if we stifle the Spirit we will miss His best in every area of life. Check which of the following ways of confirmation you have encountered:

❑ Through the Word of God—Scripture

❑ Through prayer

❑ Through the witness of other believers

❑ Through signs and wonders

❑ Through the Spirit living within me

At times, your encounter with the Holy Spirit may surprise or astound you. In those times when you face something new or unfamiliar, you may be tempted to pull back and stifle the will of God. So remember, the Holy Spirit will never hurt you. He is powerfully at work through you and will always direct you in God's best way, in God's time.

So do test every manifestation of the Spirit with God's Word and the witness of other believers, but don't stifle Him. Because not everything that is spiritual is from the Spirit of God (1 John 4:1–6). And always remember, the Spirit in you is greater than the spirit who lives in the world.

Ask Yourself . . .

❖ Is there anything you fear from the Spirit's power? If so, what is it?

❖ In what ways are you tempted to stifle the Spirit's power?

Write a prayer asking the Holy Spirit to reveal any ways you have possibly been stifling His power:

_____

_____

_____

_____

_____

W *e have proved ourselves by our purity, our understanding, our patience, our kindness, our sincere love, and the power of the Holy Spirit [holiness of the Spirit] (2 Cor. 6:6).*

The integrity of ministry is confirmed by the power of the Holy Spirit. But notice that the power of the Spirit is not the first or only confirmation. The proof of any truly Spirit-led ministry also lies in purity (holiness), understanding (of the Word), kindness and sincere love (*agape*).

So let's examine first things first. Before power comes purity, understanding, patience, kindness, and love. Put an *x* on the line of each indicating where you are spiritually right now:

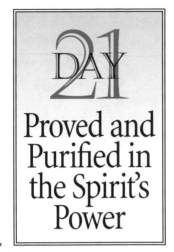

Proved and Purified in the Spirit's Power

I am . . .

Pure and holy	Impure
Understanding the Word	Not in God's Word
Patient	Impatient
Kind	Insensitive
Loving	Hateful

The Holy Spirit works in our lives to mature God's holiness in us (1 Cor. 7:1).

The Spirit uses broken, pure, and holy vessels for ministry.

The Holy Spirit may sovereignly minister to others in spite of you. To be used consistently, you must be pure and holy while bearing His fruit in honoring our Savior's name.

The Spirit manifests through holy vessels His love and powerful signs: "These signs will accompany those who believe: They will cast out demons in my name, and they will speak in new languages. They will be able to handle snakes with safety, and if they drink anything poisonous, it won't hurt them. They will be able to place their hands on the sick and heal them" (Mark 16:17–18).

Below is a list of the signs and wonders recorded in Mark 16 and Acts 1–4. Check all the proofs of the Spirit's power that you have witnessed in your life and church:

❑ The lost being saved

❑ Miracles

❑ Sick being healed

❑ Demons being cast out

❑ Speaking in tongues

❑ People being baptized and filled with the Holy Spirit

❑ Preaching the gospel with boldness

❑ Other: _____

The Holy Spirit desires to give proof of His presence in your life by demonstrating His power. But you can quench and hinder the Spirit by giving into the dictates of the flesh (1 Thess. 5:19).

Ask Yourself . . .

❖ Is anything in your life hindering the Spirit's power? Is anything you know of impure? If so, what is it? Will you confess it and surrender completely to the Holy Spirit?

❖ In what ways have you recently witnessed His power proving His presence in your life?

Write a prayer asking for Holy Spirit's power to purify you:

_____

_____

_____

_____

*H*ave you lost your senses? After starting your Christian lives in the Spirit, why are you now trying to become perfect by your own human effort? (Gal. 3:3).

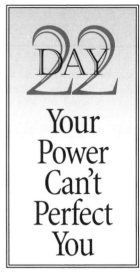

DAY 22

Your Power Can't Perfect You

Experiencing the power of the Spirit-led life can become intoxicating. But as we experience the Spirit's moving, the temptation always exists to believe that *we* can minister in signs and wonders under our *own* strength. Or, we may develop a spiritual arrogance that begins to inflict legalism on other Christians so they measure up to our "holier-than-thou" standards of piety.

The Galatians experienced the grace and power of the Holy Spirit. But they had also succumbed to the temptation of trusting in legalism instead of God's grace. They were trying to become perfect in their own efforts just as many church generations since them have done. So below is a self-test. Answer each question with a *T* for true or an *F* for false as they apply to you.

_____ I take pride in my spiritual discipline.

_____ I feel good when others praise me for my ministry in the gifts.

_____ I look for public and highly visible opportunities to use my spiritual gifts.

_____ I find myself ministering in the gifts and power of the Spirit without first seeking the leading of God's Spirit.

_____ I look for gratitude from others when I minister to them.

_____ I operate in the gifts whenever I choose.

If you found yourself marking any of the above statements true, you are treading upon thin ice spiritually. Because anytime we usurp the sovereignty of the Holy Spirit in our lives and ministry, we are reverting back to legalism and religious traditions that quench the Holy Spirit.

The only way to stop operating in our own efforts to begin moving again in the power of the Spirit is to repent of our sin. There must be the confession of our pride, arrogance, and legalistic attitudes, and ungodly actions. Pray the following prayer of repentance if vanity and arrogance is stifling your life.

Almighty God, I repent of trying to grow spiritually through my own efforts. I repent of the sins of spiritual arrogance and pride. And I ask for Your forgiveness and mercy. Cleanse me with the blood of Jesus. Purge me with the fire of Your Spirit. Crucify all pride and legalism in my life. In Jesus' name, Amen.

We will always face the temptation to manipulate the Spirit instead of surrendering to His desires. Therefore, we must always be ready to receive whatever correction, teaching, and conviction the Holy Spirit has for us through His Word, prayer, prophecy, and the fellowship of the saints.

Because we never stop needing the Spirit of grace to work pride and human effort out of our lives, complete the following sentences:

The greatest spiritual temptation I face is _____

_____.

I become spiritually arrogant when_____

_____.

I need to humble myself and repent of _____

_____.

Ask Yourself . . .

❖ Is there any area of your walk in the Spirit in which you are trying to perfect yourself through your own efforts? If so, what is it? Will you repent?

❖ How will you stay alert to avoiding the temptation to become spiritually arrogant in the future?

Write a prayer asking the Holy Spirit to convict you whenever you move from His grace to your own plans and pursuits:

_____

_____

_____

_____

_____

F or the word of God is full of living power. It is sharper than the sharpest knife, cutting deep into our innermost thoughts and desires. It exposes us for what we really are (Heb. 4:12).

DAY 23

The Spirit's Powerful Sword

Are you ready for spiritual surgery and warfare? Spiritual surgery occurs when the Holy Spirit takes the Word and cuts deep into our innermost beings, exposing who we really are. "For the word of God is full of living power. It is sharper than the sharpest knife, cutting deep into our innermost thoughts and desires. It exposes us for what we really are. Nothing in all creation can hide from him. Everything is naked and exposed before his eyes. This is the God to whom we must explain all that we have done" (Heb. 4:12–13).

And we all need the Master's knife to cut away those areas that weigh us down in sin. So do a check up. Check all the areas of your life the Holy Spirit needs to cut away with God's powerful spiritual sword. Check all that apply:

❏ My inner thoughts ❏ My habits

❏ My addictions ❏ My emotions

❏ My motives ❏ My hidden sins

❏ My prejudices ❏ My attitudes

But the sword of the Spirit is also a weapon to defeat Satan's every attack. When we wield God's sword as Jesus did during His temptation in the wilderness, the sword of the Spirit destroys the enemy's plans (Matt. 4:1–17).

> *Never reason with, debate with, or argue with Satan. Simply defeat Him with the Spirit's sword.*

But to use the sword, you must know the Word and be empowered to use it by the Spirit.

Is there anything in your life you need the Spirit to do to be ready to put on God's armor and launch an offensive attack? Underline every action you need from His Spirit now:

- ❖ Help to understand the Word

- ❖ Increased hunger and thirst for the Word

- ❖ Ability to memorize and recall the Word

- ❖ Boldness to use and apply the Word

- ❖ Strength to defeat the enemy with the Word

- ❖ Wisdom to pray the Word in and through me

Lack of use makes the Spirit's sword dull in our lives. But when we know our weapon's power, we walk in mighty power to defeat the enemy.

How well do you know the Word? Are you willing to let the Spirit do heart surgery in your life? Will you speak God's word in battle to repel the enemy's attacks?

Ask Yourself . . .

❖ Are you using the Spirit's sword?

❖ In what ways do you need to be further equipped with the sword of the Spirit?

Write a prayer asking the Holy Spirit to equip you powerfully with His sword of the Spirit—the mighty Word of God:

_____

_____

_____

_____

_____

A fter this prayer, the building where they were meeting shook, and they were all filled with the Holy Spirit. And they preached God's message with boldness (Acts 4:31).

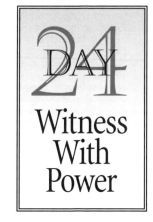

Witness With Power

The Holy Spirit empowers us to witness effectively and boldly. Like when in spite of life-threatening persecution, the early Christians told everyone, including the religious leaders, about Jesus the Messiah. "And they were all filled with the Holy Spirit. And they preached God's message with boldness" (Acts 4:31). Praying in the power of the Holy Spirit, those early Christians petitioned God, saying, "And now, O Lord, hear their threats, and give your servants great boldness in their preaching. Send your healing power; may miraculous signs and wonders be done through the name of your holy servant Jesus" (Acts 4:29–30). And their prayer literally shook the place where they were meeting, filling them with boldness!

How bold are you in witnessing for Christ? <u>Underline</u> all that apply:

Bold	Weak	Unashamed
Ashamed	Unafraid	Fearful
Excited	Lazy	Always witnessing
Rarely witnessing	Eager to share	Reluctant to share

Sharing the gospel boldly begins as you trust the Holy Spirit to give you the words to say (Luke 12:12; Matt. 10:20). So to give you some practice in sharing the gospel, complete the following sentences by letting the Holy Spirit speak through you:

God is _____.

Jesus is _____.

The Holy Spirit is _____.

Being saved is _____.

Repentance is _____.

Forgiveness is _____.

Eternal life is _____.

When you encounter the Holy Spirit you will gain a bold witness in your life.

> *Nothing another person can say or do to you should ever stop your praise and honor for the name of Jesus.*

So pray for boldness. Ask the Holy Spirit to create opportunities for you to witness daily. Determine to lead your family, friends, neighbors, work associates, and even your enemies to Jesus Christ as their Savior and Lord. Your desire for their salvation will come from your filling of the Spirit.

Ask Yourself . . .

❖ With whom should you share the gospel today?

❖ What keeps you from witnessing in power?

Write a prayer asking the Holy Spirit to give you the words to say when you are witnessing for Christ:

_____

_____

_____

_____

*T*he truth is, anyone who believes in me will do the same works I have done, and even greater works, because I am going to be with the Father. You can ask for anything in my name, and I will do it, because the work of the Son brings glory to the Father. Yes, ask anything in my name, and I will do it! (John 14:12–14).

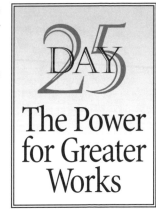

The Power for Greater Works

In this passage of John, Jesus made an astounding promise: "Anyone who believes in me will do the same works I have done, and even greater works." How is this possible? To do greater miracles, healings, deliverances, signs, and wonders than Jesus would certainly be an awesome experience. The answer: the Holy Spirit who would be sent to the disciples after Jesus left.

The source of Jesus' power was the Holy Spirit. "Then Jesus returned to Galilee, filled with the Holy Spirit's power. Soon he became well known throughout the surrounding country" (Luke 4:14). And that same Holy Spirit dwells in us and empowers us to minister as He did (Mark 16:15–20;1 Cor. 12:7). Today, through His body, the church, Jesus multiplies His ministry in the power of the Holy Spirit so that millions are saved, healed, and delivered every year.

Complete the following sentences:

Salvation miracles that I have witnessed are_____

_____.

Healing miracles that I have witnessed are_____

_____.

I have seen people set free who have been bound by_____

_____.

If you haven't witnessed God's miracle power in you or around your church, what do you think needs to happen to enable His greater works? Is there any

thing you need to yield? _____

_____

As amazing as it may sound, doing greater works—signs, wonders, and miracles—than Jesus was promised by the Lord! But we must be willing, surrendered vessels, because the Holy Spirit's power flows through humble people to work miraculously.

Ask Yourself . . .

❖ Do you believe Jesus' promise of doing great works?

❖ Are you willing to set aside pride and religious traditions in order to be used mightily by Him?

Write a prayer asking the Holy Spirit to do even greater works through you:

_____

_____

_____

_____

_____

A nd then he told them, "Go into all the world and preach the Good News to everyone, everywhere. Anyone who believes and is baptized will be saved. But anyone who refuses to believe will be condemned. These signs will accompany those who believe: They will cast out demons in my name, and they will speak new languages. They will be able to handle snakes with safety, and if they drink anything poisonous, it won't hurt them. They will be able to place their hands on the sick and heal them" (Mark 16:15–18).

DAY 26
Power for Signs and Wonders

In Mark 16, Jesus promised that those who believe in Him would be empowered to do many signs and wonders including:

- ❖ Casting out demons
- ❖ Speaking in new languages, or tongues
- ❖ Laying hands on the sick for healing

Then after the outpouring of the Holy Spirit at Pentecost, Jesus' promise became a reality. Just read the Book of Acts! In it, Luke reported that "the apostles performed many miraculous signs and wonders" which included healing the sick and casting out demons through the power of the Holy Spirit (Acts 2:43; 5:12–16; 8:4–8; 13:9–12).

Believers were never commanded by Jesus to follow signs and wonders. Rather, Jesus said signs and wonders would follow them. That is if we truly believe Jesus' words, as the apostles did. When we as believers are baptized in the power of the Holy Spirit as the disciples were commanded in Acts 1:8, we can minister like the disciples in the Spirit's gifts.

What signs and wonders have you been empowered by the Holy Spirit to use as you have ministered to others in Jesus' name? Check those you have witnessed and circle those you desire to see ministered through you:

Healings   Miracles   Deliverances

Salvations   Baptism of the Holy Spirit Prophetic Words

Discerning of Spirits

If you haven't been used in Christ's miraculous signs and wonders, why not? What does the Holy Spirit reveal to you that may be hindering His power?

The reason I have not seen signs and wonders is _____

_____ .

If the Holy Spirit manifested His power through me, I would _____

_____.

Without a belief in the Spirit's power, we will probably never see His miraculous signs released through our lives. God is sovereign, but He chooses believing vessels to move on behalf of Him.

> *When baptized in the power of the Holy Spirit, a believer becomes God's vessel for signs and wonders.*

Your focus should never be on the signs and wonders of God's miraculous power, but on the One to whom they point—Jesus Christ. As you lift Him up and serve others, signs and wonders will follow you.

Ask Yourself . . .

❖ What signs and wonders is the world seeing as the result of the Holy Spirit at work in you?

❖ How are you hindering the Spirit's power in your life?

Write a prayer yielding to the Spirit's power asking him to do anything in and through your life that Jesus Christ desires:

_____

_____

_____

_____

_____

A re any among you sick? They should call for the elders of the church and have them pray over them, anointing them with oil in the name of the Lord. And their prayer offered in faith will heal the sick, and the Lord will make them well. And anyone who has committed sins will be forgiven. Confess your sins to each other and pray for each other so that you may be healed. The earnest prayer of a righteous person has great power and wonderful results (James 5:14–16).

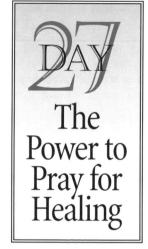

DAY 27
The Power to Pray for Healing

The Holy Spirit gives His gifts of healing to the church to heal the sick (1 Cor. 12:9). These gifts (*charismata*) of healing refer to many kinds of heal-ing—physical, emotional, and mental. Because anointing oil throughout Scripture represents the outpouring of the Holy Spirit upon a person's life, James instructed church members to call in faith for the elders of the church to pray and anoint them with oil (James 5:14).

But anointing with oil is only one way that Jesus will heal the sick. When the lame man was healed in Acts 3, Peter simply *spoke* bold words of faith in Jesus' name: "I don't have any money for you. But I'll give you what I have. In the name of Jesus Christ of Nazareth, get up and walk!" (Acts 3:6).

When addressing the religious leaders later, Peter confessed the power of Jesus' name, "The name of Jesus has healed this man—and you know how lame he was before. Faith in Jesus' name has caused this healing before your very eyes" (v. 16, 4:10).

Jesus said, "You can ask for anything in my name, and I will do it, because the work of the Son brings glory to the Father. Yes, ask anything in my name, and I will do it!" (John 14:13–14.) So whether we anoint with oil, speak powerful words, lay hands on the sick, or intercede from a distance, we must always pray and speak in Jesus' name.

List the sick people that you need to pray for and who need the elders to anoint them with oil. Write a brief healing prayer in Jesus' name next to each of their names:

Name of sick person   **Prayer**

1._____   _____

_____

2. _____   _____
                              _____

3. _____   _____
                              _____

> *The Holy Spirit will prompt you to pray in power for*
> *the sick and to seek out the gifts for their healing.*

When a sick person encounters the Holy Spirit, he or she will be led by the Spirit to go to the elders for prayer and anointing when they read James 5:14–16. Such prayer in Jesus' name stirs up faith in the church to believe God's will in healing. The same is true in the market place when we minister to the sick. So always be sensitive to the Holy Spirit's leading when you are supposed to minister or ask for healing in Jesus' name.

Ask Yourself . . .

❖ When you are sick, will you follow the leading of the Holy Spirit to ask the elders to pray for you and to anoint you with oil?

❖ Is the Spirit's power flowing through you to pray for the sick to be healed?

Write a prayer asking God's Spirit to stir up the power within you to pray for the sick:

_____

_____

_____

_____

_____

*A*fter this prayer, the building where they were meeting shook, and they were all filled with the Holy Spirit. And they preached God's message with boldness (Acts 4:31).

As the early church prayed, they were filled with the Holy Spirit, and the place where they were meeting shook with His Presence and power (Acts 4:31). Now if the building shook, those present must have also been shaken in physical, emotional, mental, and spiritual ways. Imagine the awe and wondrous power they encountered as God's Spirit shook them and filled them.

DAY 28
Shaken by the Spirit's Power

When God's Spirit shows up, both places and people may shake or tremble. Why? First, out of fear, awe, and reverence for Him. Second, the overwhelming power of His might simply causes everything in His presence to be affected physically and spiritually. Throughout Scripture both creation and people shake and tremble when in His presence.

A brief listing of passages referring to when God shook either a place or a person is given below. Write down what trembled or shook in His presence.

The Texts	Place	People
Exodus 19:18		
Judges 5:5		
Job 4:14		
Psalm 102:15		
Psalm 119:120, 161		
Isaiah 2:19–21		
Isaiah 33:4		
Isaiah 66:2		
Jeremiah 4:24		
Joel 2:1		
Habakkuk 3:16		
Haggai 2:6–7		
Matthew 27:51		

Matthew 28:4 _____ _____

Luke 8:47 _____ _____

Hebrews 12:26 _____ _____

When people shake and tremble in His presence at a church or prayer meeting, do you get offended? If you do, fix your eyes on the Lord to let Him touch you as He touches those around you.

> *Be prepared to receive in the Spirit's presence whatever manifestation He imparts to you.*

After prayer on the day of Pentecost, the Holy Spirit shook the place and filled His people. What an awesome encounter!

May your prayers be so effective that the places and the people touched by your prayers will be shaken by the power of the Holy Spirit moving through you.

Ask Yourself . . .

❖ Is the Holy Spirit shaking places and filling people through your prayers?

❖ What does the Holy Spirit need to shake by His power in your life?

Write a prayer asking the Holy Spirit to shake your life with power:

_____

_____

_____

_____

_____

I have won them over by the miracles done through me as signs from God—all by the power of God's Spirit (Rom. 15:19).

DAY 29
Won Over by Power

When the Holy Spirit manifests His power, He never intends to intimidate or overwhelm anyone. His purpose in miracles and signs is to point people to the Good News of Jesus Christ.

What are some of the feelings you have had when the power of the Spirit has been manifested? Check all that apply:

❑ Joy

❑ Intimidation

❑ Fear

❑ Excitement

❑ Filled with praise

❑ Uncomfortable

❑ Awe

❑ Filled with love for the Savior

❑ Other:

If you have had negative feelings about the power manifestations of the Holy Spirit, one of two things may be happening:

1. You may simply be uncomfortable or unfamiliar with that particular power or miracle manifestation.
2. What is being manifested is of the flesh, and is not of the Spirit of God.

Remember to test the spirits (1 John 4) and to confirm that everything which is done gives glory only to Jesus Christ. If the emphasis is on a man and not on Jesus, then the power that is manifested is in the flesh—not in the Spirit.

Listed below are some of the power manifestations of the Spirit found throughout Scripture. Check those you have encountered:

❑ The gifts of the Spirit

❑ Shaking or trembling

❑ Shouting praise

❑ Clapping in praise

❑ Singing a new song

❑ Making a joyful noise or laughter in the Spirit

❑ Falling over in the Spirit

❑ Weeping in the Spirit

❑ Other:

When the Spirit arrives in supernatural power, we may encounter His presence physically, verbally, emotionally, or mentally—all for one purpose—to point ourselves or other people to the Savior, Jesus Christ.

Ask Yourself . . .

❖ Are you willing to encounter the Spirit's power in whatever way He chooses to manifest Himself?

❖ How is the Spirit's power manifesting in your life?

Write a prayer thanking the Holy Spirit for manifesting His presence in power:

_____

_____

_____

_____

_____

T *he angel replied, "The Holy Spirit will come upon you, and the power of the Most High will overshadow you. So the baby born to you will be holy, and he will be called the Son of God"* (Luke 1:35).

As we complete our time in this series of Holy Spirit devotionals, we will look at the two most awesome displays of the Spirit's power in history: the Incarnation and the Resurrection of Jesus the Christ. If we as Christians had no other manifestations or evidences of the Holy Spirit's power, these would be enough!

DAY 30
Welcome the Spirit's Power

Take a moment to reflect in praise for the Holy Spirit's overshadowing of Mary when in that holy, miraculous moment, the Word became flesh. Now write a prayer of thanksgiving for the Holy Spirit's conceiving of Jesus in Mary:

A prayer of thanksgiving for the Incarnation

_____

_____

_____

_____

Now contemplate the Spirit's power in raising Jesus from the dead, and then write a prayer of thanksgiving for the Resurrection of Jesus the Christ:

A prayer of thanksgiving for the Resurrection

_____

_____

_____

_____

Now reflect back over the past thirty days of encountering the Spirit's power and complete these sentences:

I most need the Spirit's power _____

_____.

I encounter the Spirit's power when _____

_____.

One thing I learned about the power of the Holy Spirit that I did not know ____

_____ .

One thing I need to surrender so His power works mightily in me is _____

_____ .

Finally, we must never forget that the power of God is released into our lives by His indwelling Holy Spirit. And that we don't control Him—He controls us. That is, if we will allow Him by faith to manifest. So our part is to remain . . .

- ❖ Repentant
- ❖ Yielded
- ❖ Surrendered
- ❖ Willing
- ❖ Available to the Spirit's power!

Welcome the Spirit's power into your life!

Ask Yourself . . .

❖ Are you completely willing and eager for the Spirit's power to fill and use you?

❖ How does the Spirit desire to work powerfully through you in your family? Your church? Your world?

Write a prayer thanking God for sending His Holy Spirit in power to move through you to bless the world with the love of Jesus Christ:

_____

_____

_____

_____

_____

You can continue your encounters with the Holy Spirit by using the other devotional study guides listed at the end of this booklet, and by using the companion *Holy Spirit Encounter Bible.*

Leader's Guide

For Group Sessions

This devotional study is an excellent resource for group study including such settings as:

❖ Sunday school classes and other church classes
❖ Prayer groups
❖ Bible study groups
❖ Ministries involving small groups, home groups, and accountability groups
❖ Study groups for youth and adults

Before the First Session

❖ Contact everyone interested in participating in your group to inform them about the meeting time, date, and place.
❖ Make certain that everyone has a copy of this devotional study guide.
❖ Plan out all your teaching lessons before starting the first session. Also ask group members to begin their daily encounters in this guide. While each session will not strictly adhere to a seven-day schedule, group members who faithfully study a devotional every day will be prepared to share in the group sessions.
❖ Pray for the Holy Spirit to guide, teach, and help each participant.
❖ Be certain the place where you meet has a chalkboard, white board, or flipchart with appropriate writing materials.

Planning the Group Sessions

1. You will have four sessions together as a group. So plan to cover at least seven days in each session. If your sessions are weekly, ask the participants to complete the final two days before the last session.

2. In your first session, have group members find a partner with whom they will share and pray each time you meet. Keep the same pairs throughout the group sessions. See if you can randomly put pairs together—men with men, and women with women.

3. Have group and class members complete their devotional studies prior to their group sessions to enhance group sharing, study, and prayer. Begin each session with prayer.

4. Either the group leader or selected members should read the key Scriptures from each of the seven daily devotionals you will be studying in the session.

5. As the leader, you should decide which exercises and questions are to be covered prior to each session.

6. Also decide which exercises and sessions will be most appropriate to share with the group as a whole, or in pairs.

7. Decide which prayer(s) from the seven devotionals you will want the pairs to pray with one another.

8. Close each session by giving every group member the opportunity to share with the group how he or she encountered the Holy Spirit during the previous week. Then lead the group in prayer or have group members pray aloud in a prayer circle as you close the session.

9. You will have nine days of devotionals to study in the last session. So, use the last day as an in-depth sharing time in pairs. Invite all the group members to share the most important thing they learned about the Holy Spirit's power during this study and how their relationship with the Spirit was deepened because of it. Close with prayers of praise and thanksgiving.

10. Remember to allow each person the freedom "not to share" with their prayer partner or in public if they are uncomfortable with it.

11. Always start and end each group session on time and seek to keep them no longer than ninety minutes.

12. Finally, be careful. This is not a therapy group. Group members who seek to dominate group discussions with their own problems or questions should be ministered to by the group leader or pastor one-on-one outside of the group session.

Titles in the Holy Spirit Encounter Guide Series

Additional Notes

Additional Notes

Additional Notes

Additional Notes

Additional Notes

Additional Notes

Additional Notes

Additional Notes

Additional Notes

Additional Notes